When Faith is Weak

Reflections on trusting God and finding hope in the tough times

Tony Brown

When Faith is Weak

Onwards and Upwards Publishers
Berkeley House, 11 Nightingale Crescent,
Leatherhead, Surrey, KT24 6PD, UK
www.onwardsandupwards.org

ISBN:	978-1-907509-91-9
Typeface:	Sabon LT
Graphic design:	Leah-Maarit

To contact the author, please write to:
tonybrown43@hotmail.co.uk

About the Author

Tony Brown has been a lay preacher for forty years and has served as an elder in a Baptist church and as a member of a ministry leadership team in an Anglican church. He is a passionate believer in whole body ministry, where every member is encouraged to know their calling and exercise their gifts for the benefit and blessing of their church and community.

He has been married to Margaret for nearly thirty years. They have proved the sufficiency of God's grace in their personal struggles and in times of ill-health and bereavement. Their joint testimony is that God is faithful and reliable in all the stages of the Christian journey.

Tony's first book, 'When Faith is Weak', is written from the conviction that no experience in God's economy is ever wasted and that God is able to make something beautiful from the brokenness of our lives.

When Faith is Weak

Contents

.

Dedicated to Margaret, my
wife and soul-mate, without
whom this book would not
have been written.

Foreword

When we come up against questions and life throws up its problems – then most of us look for answers. We feel that if we can understand what is happening and why, then it may help us find a solution. If we can stop the feeling that things are out of control, then we may find some peace and, hopefully, security.

For the Christian the search for answers, meaning, peace and security involves looking at the issues and options that we have. It also involves drawing upon past experiences, Scripture and prayer. It involves the mind as well as summoning up appropriate emotions.

In this book, Tony Brown combines humour with tight argument to help us find our way. He identifies key questions and experiences, and provides Biblical insights and steps to take. His aim is not to just provide a coping strategy or simplistic answers to complex situations but to help us respond in ways that lead to maturity.

I warmly commend this practical and relevant book.

Rev. Dr. James Dainty
Chaplain to the Maranatha Community
Formerly Vicar of Christ Church, Turnham Green

"Grace means that somehow our failures and mistakes can be absorbed into God's programme. God is able to do something beautiful with the broken pieces of our lives. He meets us at those broken places where failure or sin has overtaken us, and there he brings forgiveness, healing and grace."

Preface

This book is based on three convictions. Firstly, for many of us, disappointment, setback and failure seem to characterise the Christian life rather than growth, progress and maturity. Secondly, there is hope in our battles and struggles as the grace of God is always adequate to meet our need, whatever the nature of the disappointment, the size of the setback or the extent of the failure. Thirdly, in our frailty and weakness, there is freedom to grow, scope to develop and opportunity to serve in God's great kingdom of grace.

In the ebbs and flows of life, when faith is tested and times are tough, we need to rediscover our confidence in God who patiently understands our fragility, freely forgives our sins, graciously restores our strength and lovingly lifts us to new heights of service. Each chapter of the book is concerned with a particular problem or issue that every Christian will probably confront at some point in their lives. The overriding message is that however we feel and whatever experience we face, God will never reject or abandon us but in his perfect time will bring to completion what he has begun.

There are many people who have guided and shaped my Christian life over the last fifty years. I would like to thank my parents for encouraging me in my teenage years in my membership of the Crusader movement (now Urban Saints) which laid the foundations for faith and service. My friends in Hammersmith Christian Fellowship, Borehamwood Baptist Church and Christ Church, Turnham Green have listened attentively to my sermons (and even enjoyed some of the jokes!) and in different ways have contributed to the writing of this book.

Most of all, I want to thank my wife and soul mate, Margaret, for her love, support and encouragement and for not giving up on me. The theme of this book is the range and depth of God's grace, and she has patiently exercised grace in our marriage on many occasions!

CHAPTER ONE

When We Feel Our Lives Don't Count

A man was driving along a country road when he had to swerve to avoid an oncoming car. As he turned the wheel, he realised that he had hit something and stopped the car to investigate. He found a rabbit-like animal lying motionless by the side of the car. Just then, another driver pulled up behind him and asked what was wrong. The other man pointed to the animal and said, "I've just run it over and it's not moving."

The second man had a look and said, "I think I can help." He went to his car and took out a bottle and poured the contents over the animal. After a minute or two, the rabbit-like creature got up and ran. But every few yards he stopped to wave at the two people. It ran, stopped and waved, ran, stopped and waved. And this went on until it disappeared from their view.

"That's amazing!" said the first man. "What was in the bottle?"

The other man showed it to him, and on the label it said "Hair restorer, with a permanent wave."

We all have stories to tell – not just what happened last week, yesterday or today, but our life story, and an important part of that narrative is the story of our journey of faith. What matters is how our story connects with God's story and how we can become part of that greater story in building God's kingdom.

Every church also has a story – there are times of growth and joy and there are times of setback and disappointment. But it is not a finished story as God has more to do in advancing his kingdom through his people. We all have a different story of faith, and yet through the witness of the church these stories combine to tell people that God is alive and at work in his world.

The reality of the story

Some stories are true and others are fiction. God's story of redemption is real, relevant and reliable. It tells of his great love for the world and how Jesus came to live among us, identify with our humanity, enter into our suffering and die on a cross to save us from our sins.

God writes the story but as Christians we are part of it. Our experiences are real – they cannot be denied or devalued. No one can take away our story or contradict it. We know that God has spoken through his word, forgiven us, guided our decisions, answered prayer, intervened on our behalf, provided for us, protected us and reassured us in times of confusion or doubt.

If you ask people about the meaning of life, some may answer there is no meaning – or if there is, it is hidden from us. Some may believe in fate or chance to explain why things happen, but really that is no explanation at all. Fate suggests that the story has been written in advance and we cannot change it, influence or shape it. "Que sera, sera; whatever will be, will be…"

According to this view, we are merely doing what has been decided already – but by whom or what? Are we the players following a script and acting out a plot that has been written and settled? Has everything been determined from the beginning of time? And what is the reference point for when time began? Are we predestined to behave as we do? If we are, why try to change or improve anything, why protest against injustice, why campaign against evil? Where is the incentive and where is the hope that we can make a difference in our world?

What about chance? Does life consist of a series of random events, where there is no rhyme or reason, no pattern or purpose? Things just happen because they happen. It's a matter of luck. Or Christians may use the word 'fortunate' when something good happens or something bad is avoided! But when we refer to luck or chance we can usually find a cause for the effect that we see, and often human agency is involved. Events have causes, connections and consequences. A lucky goal in football is the result of a player being in the right position. There was a natural explanation for the accident to the hare in the opening story.

We live in a regular and not a random universe, where natural and spiritual laws are in operation. If you boil an egg for ten minutes, you are likely to get a hard-boiled egg. But what caused it? You, the oven, the gas or electricity you used? All are contributory causes, although human agency is needed to start the process.

Pharaoh is a good example of a spiritual law. We read that he "hardened his heart" (Exodus 8:15,32). We also find that God hardened his heart (Exodus 9:12,10:20). Both statements are true. It is a spiritual law that if you continue to reject God, and refuse to listen to his voice, you will become more stubborn and resistant to him.

Fate says that the story has been written in advance and that we have no contribution to make to the scheme of things. Chance suggests there is no overarching story and whatever narrative we write is unconnected with anything else and our lives are irrelevant and inconsequential.

But the truth is that we are part of a real story, God's story, and there are more chapters to be written.

The richness of the story

What makes a convincing and compelling story? We may have to suspend our disbelief, of course! A good story needs to hold our attention and capture our imagination so that we are drawn into the story. It requires an unfolding and developing plot (and sometimes sub-plots), interesting and complex characters, twists and turns in the story, and a few surprises to keep us guessing.

We are part of a rich story. Our story of faith is rich because it has variety, colour, depth, truth and reality. It has been formed and shaped by a range and diversity of experiences – often in tough and painful times. And it is a continuing and developing story which speaks of God's grace in bringing change and transformation to often stubborn and resistant hearts. We are work in progress!

The Bible tells many stories of people who sometimes got it right and at other times got it wrong. They messed up, just as we do. Their frailties and weaknesses are openly displayed – jealousy, deception, corruption, plotting, political manoeuvring, rebellion, relationship failure, family breakdown. Men and women of faith had their doubts, temptations and struggles yet they are part of God's story of rescuing and redeeming a fallen humanity and recreating a broken world.

King David knew the depths of God's mercy when he sinned and took responsibility for his behaviour

(Psalm 51). But he also affirmed the parallel truth of God's foreknowledge:

Psalm 139:13-16
For you created my inmost being; ... All the days ordained for me were written in your book before one of them came to be.

God's foreknowledge does not deny our freedom to make choices and decisions. We are not puppets controlled by divine strings or robots operated by heavenly levers. We are not the pieces on a cosmic chess board which have been programmed to move in a certain way and direction.

The story of Jonah, which we will consider in chapter 5, illustrates how God does not override or restrict our freedom to make mistakes but works in and through our circumstances to fulfil his purpose and plan. He does not reject us, abandon us or disqualify us for future service. God told Jonah to take a message to the people of Nineveh and he ran away. He was thrown overboard by the sailors because they were afraid and thought it was his fault that a fierce storm developed. God provided a great fish to rescue him and gave him a second opportunity to go to Nineveh.

God allowed Jonah to run. He did not force him to go to Nineveh. But he brought him back into his purpose and will. God in his mercy and grace accommodates our failures and mistakes. This does not mean we can live as we like and get away with things. There are consequences for our actions and behaviour.

It would have been unpleasant being inside the fish for three days and nights! If we experience the discipline of God, it may be for a while but it is for our good and is designed to bring us closer to him so that we can be used again (see Hebrews 12:7-11).

When we run from God, he finds us and meets us to repair the damage caused by sin and to restore us to wholeness. He lifts us out of sin and sadness to new heights of life and faith so that we can continue to tell the story of his love and grace. In the economy of God no experience is ever wasted, however adverse, negative, ugly or painful it may be.

In the next chapter, we see in the story of Joseph how the harmful intentions of his brothers were turned to good and resulted in a great deliverance for his family and the people of Egypt. God takes the failures, the mistakes, the pain, the suffering, the hurts, the disappointments and includes them in his story – in his bigger story of saving and reconciling a broken world and in our personal stories of forgiveness and grace. It's a rich story, full of meaning, purpose and hope.

The reading of the story

We are not all called to be evangelists but all of us are called to be witnesses. A witness tells of what they have seen, heard or experienced. The Great Commission of Jesus (Matthew 28:18-20) tells us to "make disciples of all nations", and disciples cannot be made unless they hear the gospel and see it in action.

17

We all have our own story of faith, our personal journey with God, which we can share with others. Every story is true and personal – the story of what God has done and the changes he has brought about in our lives.

2 Corinthians 3:2-3
You yourselves are our letter, written on our hearts, known and read by everybody. You show that you are a letter from Christ, the result of our ministry, written not with ink but with the Spirit of the living God, not on tablets of stone but on tablets of human hearts.

People are reading our story and through us are reading God's story. We have a part in the writing of that story, not only through what we say but how we live. Every prayer, every offer of forgiveness, every expression of mercy, every relationship rebuilt, every gift of grace and every act of service advances the kingdom of God and brings more people into the story.

Writing about Job's suffering, Philip Yancey says:

"...His struggle presents a glimpse of what the Bible elsewhere spells out in detail: the remarkable truth that our choices matter, not just to us and our own destiny but, amazingly, to God himself and the universe he rules ... Every act of faith by every one of the people of God is

like the tolling of a bell, and a faith like Job's reverberates throughout the universe."[1]

God's story is about rescuing, redeeming and reconciling a fallen humanity and a broken world. As individual Christians and collectively as people of faith we have a part in that story, and our contribution can shape the story by the choices and decisions we make. We all mess up at times. We get it wrong. We miss what God is saying. We don't join in with what he is doing. This happens in church life too. But the story is not finished. God is able to blend our failures and mistakes into his plan and use them for our good and for the blessing of others.

Our lives do count. We can be an influence for God where we are. You may know the story of the boy and the starfish. Millions of these fish were stranded on a beach early in the morning. They would die if left until the morning sun. A boy was picking them up, one by one, and throwing them back into the sea.

A man noticed what he was doing and said to him, "The beach goes on for miles, and there are millions of starfish. How can you make any difference?"

The boy looked at the starfish in his hand and said, "It makes a difference to this one."

We can make a difference by the way that we live and the contribution we make to the narrative that God

---

[1] Taken from *Disappointment with God* by Philip Yancey. Copyright © 1988 by Philip Yancey. Used by permission of Zondervan. www.zondervan.com

is writing. We do not need fate, chance or luck to explain why things happen. We are part of a real story of God at work changing and transforming lives by his grace and power, telling a rich story of what God has done for us and presenting that story to others to read so that they too may join the greatest story ever told.

CHAPTER TWO

When We Find It Hard To Forgive

A group of children were asked, "What do we have to do before we receive forgiveness?"

One bright spark answered, "Sin!"

A related and equally important question is this: "Should repentance come before forgiveness, or does God ask us to forgive those who don't repent of their sin?" In seeking an answer to this second question, we need to consider the essence and effects of forgiveness. What does it mean to forgive? And what does forgiveness do?

First of all, we need to clear up a possible misunderstanding about this issue. In thinking about God's forgiveness, it is sometimes believed that his mercy overrides his justice. But God is able to extend mercy to us because his justice was wholly satisfied on the cross. Jesus paid the full price and penalty for our sin when he died on our behalf and in our place. Paul expresses the truth like this:

> **Romans 3:25-26**
> *God presented Christ as a sacrifice of atonement, through the shedding of his blood – to be received by faith ... he did it to demonstrate his righteousness at the present time, so as to be just and the one who justifies those who have faith in Jesus.*

The command and challenge for Christians is to forgive unreservedly those who have sinned against us. Every time we say the Lord's Prayer, we link our forgiveness from God with the forgiveness we show to others: "Forgive us our debts, as we also have forgiven our debtors." (Matthew 6:12)

Debts may be created in relationships by imposing obligations on others to satisfy us when we have been hurt or offended. There was a man who had lived an immoral life and had run up huge debts who started going to church.

"I've given up sin," he said to the vicar one Sunday.

"That's good," replied the vicar, "and are you going to pay all your debts as well?"

"Now wait a minute," the man protested, "you're not talking about religion now – you're talking about business!"

Forgiveness refines our reactions

The principles of forgiveness are illustrated well in the life of Joseph. He was his father's favourite and his brothers were jealous of him, and they were upset even more by his dreams about his superiority. They hatched a plan to sell him to some merchants who were going to Egypt to trade, and they, in turn, sold him to Potiphar, the captain of Pharaoh's guard. We read that the Lord was with him and he was promoted to run the household. Then, after a failed attempt by Mrs Potiphar to seduce him, and her false accusation, he ended up in prison (Genesis 37, 39).

On the face of it, Joseph had reason to withhold forgiveness from his brothers who had set in motion the chain of events which led to his imprisonment for thirteen years. But God was at work in him while he was there. He was being softened, refined, moulded, matured and prepared for future use. The pride and arrogance had to go to make room for compassion and concern. Although Joseph could not see the whole picture or understand the purposes of God at this stage, he trusted him for the outcome. Instead of becoming hard and bitter, he learned the art of forgiveness in prison.

In realising how much God has forgiven us, and recognising our own sin, we become more sensitive to the weaknesses and failures of others. In the process of working through forgiveness, we begin to understand something of what God is teaching us and showing us about our character and our need to change. Forgiveness refines our reactions as we allow God to heal our hurts and trust him to bring his purposes to fulfilment even if, like Joseph, we cannot see it immediately.

Forgiveness releases our resentment

Pharaoh was troubled by dreams concerning feast and famine, and after Joseph interpreted them he was released from prison and restored to favour. He became the governor of Egypt with responsibility for controlling the food supply and ensuring that stores were accumulated in the good years to cover the years of famine. Because the famine was not confined to Egypt, Joseph's brothers came to find food. Joseph interviewed them, and although he pretended not to recognise them it is evident that he had forgiven them. He provided for their journey home and returned their money (Genesis 42).

Our natural reaction when we have been wronged is to retaliate, to be seen to be right, to be justified or to be vindicated. The energy channelled into getting even is self-destructive. It has been said that holding a grudge is like letting someone live rent free in your head![2] Forgiveness releases us and releases the person who has hurt or offended us. When we start praying for

[2] From *A Bundle of Laughs* by J. John and Mark Stibbe. Copyright © J. John and Mark Stibbe 2005. Monarch Books. Used by permission.

someone and ask God to bless that person, something is unlocked inside us. We are released because the resentment that blocks our forgiveness is removed and replaced with grace to reach out to others. The person who has wronged or hurt us is freed from the need to find out the conditions under which they may be forgiven.

Our natural reaction may be to think, "I'll forgive them when I'm ready. I can forgive but I can't forget. Let them stew for a while. There are lessons to be learned. They must not conclude that forgiveness is easy. They need to consider the extent of the pain they have caused by their words or actions. They must show signs of repentance."

But what did Jesus say?

Matthew 6:14-15
For if you forgive men when they sin against you, your heavenly Father will also forgive you. But if you do not forgive men their sins, your Father will not forgive your sins.

The principle is plain to see. If we refuse to forgive, delay forgiveness or set conditions for forgiveness we reduce our own capacity to be forgiven. By practising forgiveness we enlarge our capacity to receive forgiveness.

When Jesus looked down from the cross at those who had crucified him, people for whom he died, he said, "Father, forgive them, for they do not know what

25

they are doing." (Luke 23:34) Jesus chose to forgive. And so must we.

This is not about feelings or human reactions. It is a matter of the will, and we need God's help and grace to do it. But it can have powerful consequences. Only the grace and power of God can move a parent to forgive those who attacked their son or daughter or lead someone to seek reconciliation with those responsible for the death of family members or friends.

Nor is this about natural justice which must take its course when the law has been broken. Forgiveness has a spiritual nature and quality but does not mean that someone thereby escapes the legal penalty for what they have done. But the exercise of forgiveness may cause a person to reflect on their behaviour and to admit their need to change direction and seek God for themselves.

Practising forgiveness is obedience to God's word and living out the truths of the gospel – a message of reconciliation through the redeeming sacrifice of Jesus on the cross. Forgiveness releases resentment when we let go of the hurt and let God do his work.

Forgiveness rebuilds our relationships

At the end of the story, Jacob died and Joseph's brothers were worried that he might repay them for the way they had treated him.

Genesis 50:16-17
So they sent word to Joseph, saying, "Your father left these instructions before he died: This is what

you are to say to Joseph: I ask you to forgive
your brothers the sins and the wrongs they
committed in treating you so badly. Now please
forgive the sins of the servants of the God of your
father." When their message came to him, Joseph
wept.

The brothers' request for forgiveness was based on self-interest. But it did not prevent Joseph from demonstrating true forgiveness. He was not their judge and he knew how God had worked to bring about a higher purpose and a greater plan.

Genesis 50:19-21
But Joseph said to them, "Don't be afraid. Am I
in the place of God? You intended to harm me,
but God intended it for good to accomplish what
is now being done, the saving of many lives. So
then, don't be afraid. I will provide for you and
your children." And he reassured them and spoke
kindly to them.

How do we forgive? Paul tells us in his letter to the Colossian Christians: "Forgive as the Lord forgave you." (Colossians 3:13b) How has God forgiven us? Fully, freely, finally. The parable of the unmerciful servant (Matthew 18:21-35) illustrates the principle of unlimited forgiveness. This begins in the heart. For relationships to be rebuilt, forgiveness must be received. Our attitude to someone who has wronged us may soften their resistance and move them towards repentance, but only God is able to change the heart.

The way that Joseph forgave his brothers and the grace he showed them reminds us of how God treats us – not according to our sin but according to his mercy. And this is how we should treat others who sin against us.

Forgiveness refines our reactions if we allow God to soften our hearts when we have been hurt by others and trust him to work out the best outcome.

Forgiveness releases our resentment when we let go of grudges and the desire to get back at someone and instead ask God to bless them.

Forgiveness rebuilds relationships when we seek to be reconciled with those who have wronged us, if they are prepared for the relationship to be restored.

In some circumstances these steps are cumulative and the potential for change in others comes after change has occurred in us. But one thing is clear: only God can move the heart to repentance (Romans 2:4). So, to answer the question posed at the beginning of the chapter, our forgiveness is not conditional and dependent on it being accepted. There are two aspects – the benefit and blessing for the forgiver and for the person who receives that forgiveness. Only God knows the heart and whether there is true and genuine repentance, which enables the gift of forgiveness to be fully enjoyed. But it is clear that we should not look for repentance first or require a change in behaviour in advance before we forgive those who have wronged us.

CHAPTER THREE

When God Seems Far Away

There is a verse in the book of Isaiah that we may find particularly hard to understand: "Truly you are a God who hides himself, O God and Saviour of Israel." (45:15)

But surely God is knowable? He has revealed himself to us in creation, in history, in his word and in Jesus. As we look around us, we observe the characteristics of a Creator, who planned and designed and shaped the world for our use and enjoyment. His intervention in history demonstrates his concern for his creation and his desire to bring people into relationship with him. We understand the progressive revelation of God in his word as he gradually unfolds his nature and purposes through Genesis to Revelation.

In Jesus we see the full and final revelation of God, for Jesus the Son has all the attributes and qualities of God the Father and has his perfect likeness.

Colossians 2:9
For in Christ all the fulness of the Deity lives in bodily form.

Hebrews 1:3
The Son is the radiance of God's glory and the exact representation of his being...

Then we come across the verse in Isaiah that seems to contradict what we know about God.

A common experience

It is good to ask questions. A father and his son went fishing. The boy was curious about the world around him.

He said to his father, "Dad, how does this boat float?"

"I don't know, son," Dad replied.

"Dad, do fish breathe underwater?" was the next question.

"I'm not sure, son," Dad answered.

Then the boy asked, "Dad, why is the sky blue?"

"I really don't know the answer to that," was the reply.

"Dad, you don't mind me asking all these questions do you?"

"Of course not, son," said Dad. "How else are you going to learn anything?"

Psalm 42 will help us, as we see the writer struggling with his feelings about God when he does not enjoy the closeness and joy of his presence. The writer to this Psalm asks himself a question: "Why are you downcast, O my soul?" A downcast soul is a common experience in the Christian life. If we are honest, there are times when it seems that God hides himself from us. He seems far away, he does not act or intervene, and there appears to be no answer to our prayers. God is silent. He has withdrawn his presence from us – or so it seems.

These concerns are seen elsewhere in the Psalms. Where is God? Why is he far from me? Has he forgotten me? Has he abandoned me? Will I find him again? We think too of the words of Jesus on the cross: "My God, my God, why have you forsaken me?" (Matthew 27:46). Jesus was separated temporarily from the presence of his Father as he bore the weight of our sin and guilt in his perfect body.

There are seasons of the soul. Just as our outlook and moods are affected by contrasts and changes in the weather during the year, so our attitude and feelings reflect the variety and variability of our circumstances. In the Christian journey, faith is tested and tried in times of hardship, confusion and suffering when prayers are not immediately answered and God seems distant and unresponsive.

So we need to be able to handle the silence of God and trust him in times of doubt, darkness and even despair. God uses these experiences to strengthen our faith, develop our character, bring us to maturity and make us more like Jesus. We have not been rejected or abandoned by God in these times when he seems to be far away. He is teaching us trust and dependence through lessons of faith and obedience.

God wants us to be honest and real with him. We see this reflected in the Psalms, when the writers pour out their hearts to God. They do not pretend all is well when life is falling apart and they have come to an end of their own resources. They express their concerns, anxieties, feelings and fears. They tell God why they are hurting. And so should we. Our God is a loving and compassionate Father who allows only what he can use.

So what does the Psalmist do?

A comforting exercise

Psalm 42:6

My soul is downcast within me; therefore I will remember you...

Memory is very useful. The conductor Sir Thomas Beecham attended a prestigious reception and was in conversation with someone he recognised but whose name he could not recall. He began the conversation, desperate to find a clue to the person's identity.

"So are you well?"

"Yes, thank you."

"And the family?"

"Yes, they are fine."

"And your husband, is he well?"

"Yes, very well, thank you."

"And is he still in the same line of business?"
"Yes, he's still king."[3]

The writer to the Psalms uses his memory, his personal bank of knowledge and experience, to remind himself of the goodness and faithfulness of God. He recalls specific acts and times where God has moved and worked – in the nation, in history and in his own life. This is a good practice to follow.

No one can take from us or deny the ways in which God has spoken to us in the past or intervened on our behalf. We can recall particular events and times when we knew that it was God at work and not a coincidence or chance happening. So when God seems to be distant or we cannot hear his voice we should focus on the good things he has done by calling to mind evidence of his unconditional and unchanging love.

What we have learned and experienced of God in the light will also help us in the dark. We are work in progress. There will be no unfinished symphonies in heaven! Paul reminds us that what God has commenced he will continue and what he continues he will finish:

Philippians 1:6
...he who began a good work in you will carry it on to completion until the day of Christ Jesus.

---

[3] From *A Bundle of Laughs* by J. John and Mark Stibbe. Copyright © J. John and Mark Stibbe 2005. Monarch Books. Used by permission.

As well as trusting the good purposes of God, we must also rely on his sure promises. We may be out of fellowship with him and need to come to him for cleansing and forgiveness. This may not be the reason why God seems absent or remote but may be a possible explanation. If the devil accuses us of sin, we know what to do and where we should go. "Call yourself a Christian? Look at what you have just done!" We come to our heavenly Father, who forgives us freely and restores the relationship broken by sin. We trust in the promises of God that there is no condemnation for the Christian and that the blood of Jesus goes on cleansing from all sin (Romans 8:1-2, 1 John 1:9).

There may be times when God seems distant although our desire is to be close to him and to know him more. We seek to live in accordance with his word and to walk in his will. God may use these experiences to call us to a deeper level of trust and commitment to prepare and equip us for future service. As faith is stretched it becomes stronger and is patient when there is no direct evidence of God's activity. When we cannot sense his presence, and we feel he is not speaking to us, then we need to hold on to the reliability of his word and the security of his promises. He will never leave us or abandon us, whatever circumstances or feelings may suggest (Hebrews 13:5b).

A comforting exercise is to recall God's faithfulness and rest in his good purposes and promises. These reassure us that he has not finished with us and will bring to fulfilment his desire that we become more like his Son Jesus.

A confident expression

The Psalmist writes:

Psalm 42:11b
Put your hope in God, for I will yet praise him, my Saviour and my God.

It is good to speak to ourselves, to command our soul to praise the Lord. "Bless the Lord, O my soul!" This is a matter of the will and not the feelings, which are not a reliable indicator or barometer of spiritual health. Feelings are changeable and often dependent on outward circumstances. Worship is affirming the worthiness of God. He is worthy of our worship whether we face internal tensions or external pressures.

The expression used here by the Psalmist may also be understood in another way: "I'm having difficulty now but the time will come when I will praise the Lord again. I will put my hope in God and I will yet praise him."

Our confidence is not in ourselves. It is not the result of us reflecting on our lives and concluding that we are not doing so badly after all. It is not about being positive about things or putting on a brave face. Nor is it a denial of what is happening and a refusal to face up to the realities of life and the fact that we live in a fallen and suffering world.

Our confidence comes from knowing God and that he will always be true to his word and never act in a way inconsistent with his nature and character. Our confidence is in a God who is absolutely faithful and reliable. Our confidence is based on having proved God at different times and in a variety of circumstances. Our confidence tells us that we will praise him again.

It is a common experience to feel at times that God is far away. But it is a comforting exercise to recall his goodness and faithfulness. And we can confidently express the truth that he will be close again.

Psalm 42:11 (TLB)
But O my soul, don't be discouraged. Don't be upset. Expect God to act! For I know that I shall again have plenty of reason to praise him for all that he will do. He is my help! He is my God!

CHAPTER FOUR

When Our Plans Fall Apart

Dealing with disappointment is something we all have to face, probably at different points in our lives. Disappointment arises when our hopes are not fulfilled or our expectations are not realised, whether in relationships, family life, employment or church. Perhaps something we set our heart on has not happened or someone we trusted has let us down. And disappointment may be accompanied by a sense of failure, if we feel responsible for the situation or that we have contributed to it in some way.

How do we handle disappointment, when our plans fall apart? How do we come to terms with it and work through it? How do we discern what God is saying to us?

In 2 Samuel 7, we find that David was disappointed when his wish to build a temple was refused by God.

A PROPER DESIRE

David's motives were sound and his intentions were good. There do not appear to be any elements of self or pride in his desire. David loved God and had a personal and intimate relationship with him. From this relationship came a genuine desire to build a temple which would be the centre for the worship of God. This desire was commended by God:

> **2 Chronicles 6:8**
> *But the Lord said to my father David, "Because it was in your heart to build a temple for my Name, you did well to have this in your heart."*

A PERSONAL DISAPPOINTMENT

Although Nathan the prophet initially encouraged David to carry out his plan (2 Samuel 7:3), God revealed to him that it was not his will for David to construct the temple. He did not say that it should not be built but that David would not be the one to do it. The explanation was that David was a warrior and the building of the temple would coincide with a period of peace (see 1 Chronicles 22:6-10).

A POSITIVE DECISION

David took his disappointment to God (2 Samuel 7:18-29). In his prayer he...

- ...acknowledges God's sovereignty (v.22)
- ...affirms God's faithfulness (vs.23-24)

- ...accepts God's will for him (vs.28-29)

So what can we learn from David's reaction to his disappointment at not being able to build the temple?

The will of God must always be sought first. We may have a good idea but it may be our own idea. We may have a godly desire but we should not make assumptions or draw conclusions about what we think God has decided. This is not to suggest that thinking and reasoning are not required in the preparation, planning and execution of an initiative or venture. What is important is to check and confirm our plans with God, so that our will is aligned with his will.

Like Nathan, we may be encouraged by other people in our service for God, but we should not rely on them for confirmation of a decision. They may be well-intentioned but may be wrong. This is not to say that we should ignore the wise counsel of other Christians, but ultimately guidance should be tested by God's word and the leading of the Holy Spirit.

It is also necessary to distinguish between the immediate purposes of God, concerned with the here and now, and his wider purposes relating to the future. David wanted to build a house for God. But God responded by saying he would give David a house (1 Chronicles 17:25). Jesus came from David's line, and through this promise there would be salvation for the world (see Luke 1:32-33).

It is possible for us to be so preoccupied with our own disappointment that we do not see what God is doing. Or we may have invested so much in something that our hopes and dreams are shattered when it does not materialise. It is important then, as an act of faith, to transfer our focus to God and allow him to determine the way forward. Trusting in God means that although we may not see the bigger picture, we can be confident in his power to secure the right outcome. It's not about our credibility or vindication – it's about the success of God's work and seeing him get the glory.

When circumstances do not work out as we expect we need to remember that God has other plans. The task of building the temple was given to Solomon (2 Chronicles 6:9). It was God's will that the construction be completed by him. The work of building God's kingdom continues through other people or other methods when our ideas, desires or plans do not come to fruition.

But even though our desire may not be granted, or given in the form we seek, it does not follow that we are excluded from God's purposes. It does not mean we cannot be used again or used elsewhere. David had a contribution to make to the work. He chose the site for the construction scheme, drew up the plans and provided the materials. He was actively involved with it, although it was not his personal project and he would not live to see it finished (see 1 Chronicles 28:12,19). He gave generously from his own resources and encouraged others to give as an expression of their commitment to God (1 Chronicles 29:1-9).

In life there are disappointments and setbacks. We fail and fall. We get things wrong. We misunderstand God's will. We may persuade ourselves that something is right, for the best of reasons, and yet be mistaken. We may be disappointed in our expectations concerning other people.

The answer is to follow David's example and take our concerns to God, reminding ourselves that he is in absolute control and his will is best. By resting too in God's faithfulness, and trusting in his good promises and purposes, we find confidence and security. However circumstances turn out, God is never a disappointment.

Jeremiah 29:11
"For I know the plans I have for you," declares the Lord, "plans to prosper you and not to harm you, plans to give you hope and a future."

CHAPTER FIVE

When We Try To Escape From God

There was a Christian woman who travelled frequently, and she always took her Bible to read on the plane. On one flight she sat next to a man who, when he saw her take out her Bible, gave a little chuckle and went back to what he was doing.

After a while, he turned to her and asked, "You don't believe all that stuff in there, do you?"

The woman replied, "Of course I do. It is the word of God."

He said, "Well, what about that guy who was swallowed by a whale?"

She replied, "Oh, Jonah. Yes I believe that; it is in the Bible."

He asked, "Well, how do you suppose he survived all that time inside the whale?"

She said, "I don't really know. I guess when I get to heaven, I will ask him."

"What if he isn't in heaven?" the man asked sarcastically.

The woman replied, "Then you can ask him."

While some dismiss the story of Jonah as being untrue, others see it as a myth with useful lessons to learn. But is it just a fishy tale about a man who was down in the mouth? There is a reference to Jonah son of Amittai, the prophet from Gath Hepher, in 2 Kings 14:25. Jesus regarded Jonah as an historical person and the events recorded about Nineveh as real.

Matthew 12:40-41
For as Jonah was three days and three nights in the belly of a huge fish, so the Son of Man will be three days and three nights in the heart of the earth. The men of Nineveh will stand up at the judgment with this generation and condemn it; for they repented at the preaching of Jonah, and now one greater then Jonah is here.

So we should treat this account as accurate and authentic. It's a great story. Jonah is hardly a role model but we can identify with him. The book illustrates the truth that you can run from God but not hide from him. We discover something of the nature and character of God, his purpose and power, his provision and protection.

An important theme is God's discipline of his people. This is redemptive, remedial and restorative. It is proof of God's ownership and evidence of his love (Hebrews 12:6). It is a sign of his grace and an expression of his mercy. It is not about punishment for our sin, for Jesus died in our place on the cross bearing the judgment and penalty for sin that we deserved.

So the purpose of God's correction is not to hurt but to heal, not to bind but to bless, not to restrict but to release. The book is about confidence and hope in God, looking forward to "one greater than Jonah" – to Jesus, God's only Son, who reveals the Father's love to us and rescues us from sin by dying on the cross on our behalf and rising to give us new life.

Overtaken by failure

God spoke to Jonah:

Jonah 1:2
"Go to the great city of Nineveh and preach against it, because its wickedness has come up before me."

Jonah ran in the opposite direction! He found a ship that was conveniently bound for Tarshish where he was heading. He was thrown overboard by the sailors when he admitted that he was running from God and was responsible for the violent storm that was buffeting the ship. God rescued him by preparing, or providing, a great fish to swallow him. In the belly of the fish Jonah came to his spiritual senses.

Jonah 3:1-2
*Then the word of the Lord came to Jonah a
second time: "Go to the great city of Nineveh
and proclaim to it the message I give you."*

Having been battered by the storm, grilled by the
sailors, and swallowed and regurgitated by the fish,
Jonah didn't argue!

The word of the Lord came a second time. God
could have bypassed Jonah. He could have found
someone else to go to Nineveh. Or he could have sent
Jonah home for more training. But God not only had
work to do for Jonah, he had work to do *in* Jonah.

Thank God for second opportunities! Thank God
for the second word! We may be reluctant to do what
God has asked of us – perhaps to speak to someone
about our faith or to offer forgiveness when we have
been hurt – because we are unsure of how it will be
received. God disciplines us in love when we don't hear
him speaking or we decide to ignore him or go our own
way. But Jonah tells us that failure is not final.
Whatever our failure, whatever our sin, whatever we
have done, there is a word from God for us. Like
Jonah, the way back to God, and the way forward with
God, is through repentance. This means agreeing with
God, admitting we are wrong and being willing to
change and be changed.

Jonah discovered that God is not only just and
merciful but also gracious. Justice is giving us what we
deserve. Mercy is holding back what we deserve. But
grace is giving us what we do not deserve. If someone

steals your car and you want to see the thief prosecuted, that's justice. If you are content just to get your car back and not see the thief charged, that's mercy. But if you give the thief the car, that's grace!

God redeems the past by his grace. This means that today need not be controlled by yesterday, that the sins of the past need not immobilise us, that the guilt of the past need not paralyse us, and that the hurts of the past need not crush us. By his grace, there is no sin that cannot be forgiven, no guilt that cannot be removed, no failure that cannot be redeemed and no hurt that cannot be healed.

Grace means that somehow our failures and mistakes can be absorbed into God's programme. God is able to do something beautiful with the broken pieces of our lives. He meets us at those broken places where failure or sin has overtaken us, and there he brings forgiveness, healing and grace. In these areas of weakness and frailty he begins to rebuild our confidence and faith. He uses our experiences, including the negative circumstances, to develop a closer relationship with him and a greater dependence on him.

Overwhelmed by feelings

After Jonah had preached, the people repented and God had compassion on them. But was Jonah pleased? We find him sulking in chapter 4. He says to God, in effect, "I knew it! I told you so!" He knew that God would forgive the people of Nineveh if they turned to him and that's why he didn't go the first time.

He was more concerned about God exercising judgment than extending mercy. He wanted to be proved right, to be justified, to be vindicated. So he "waited to see what would happen to the city." (4:5)

God deals with him gently and challenges him about his assumptions and attitudes about the people of Nineveh: "Have you any right to be angry?" (4:4) We would say, "Pull yourself together! Get a grip! Stop feeling sorry for yourself!"

God understands our struggles, uncertainties, anxieties and fears. He wants us to be honest and open with him. He can handle our questions and doubts. A good father does not turn away his children when they are troubled. Our perfect heavenly Father wants his children to come to him as they are with all their frailties, imperfections, inconsistencies and contradictions.

Then we see how Jonah was grateful for the vine that protected him from the sun, and angry when the vine withered and the sun blazed on him. Notice how his feelings change. In verse 9 he is angry again!

We are influenced and at times controlled by our feelings. They are important. We are people with emotions. But as noted in chapter 3, feelings are not a reliable indicator of spiritual health. They can mislead us or misrepresent the problem. So we should not derive our security from feelings or circumstances or draw unwarranted conclusions from them. God wanted

Jonah to trust him and not depend on the vine that gave him temporary comfort. Feelings are fallible and changeable. They may overwhelm us but there is an answer and an antidote.

Overcoming through faith

1 John 5:4b
This is the victory that has overcome the world, even our faith.

It is not the size of our faith that matters but where our faith is located – in a powerful and almighty God.

Faith is not unreasonable, a gigantic leap in the dark. Faith rests on substantial historical evidence. Scientific enquiry and archaeological investigation have given valuable insights into God's creative activities and intervention in our world. Historical research has demonstrated the reliability and trustworthiness of the New Testament documents. When Paul writes about the reality of the resurrection of Jesus, he appeals to certain incontrovertible facts (1 Corinthians 15:3-8). Faith is the entrusting of ourselves to a faithful God who has proved to be true to his word and who has not failed us in the past.

Jonah demonstrated his faith while in the fish. "I remembered you, Lord, and my prayer rose to you ... Salvation comes from the Lord." (2:7-9)

We may be overtaken by failure or overwhelmed by feelings but faith overcomes because God hears us when we cry to him. He answers our prayer, he speaks to us in our need, he forgives our sin, he restores our relationship, he reassures us of his love, he intervenes in our circumstances, and he reinstates us in his service.

The God of Jonah is our God, and one greater than Jonah – Jesus – is here.

CHAPTER SIX

When We Are Running on Empty

There are probably times when we have all taken a deep breath before saying something that we think may not be received too well. A conversation between a man and his wife went like this:

He said to her, "You're in a bad mood. What's the matter with you?"

"Nothing."

"Is it something I said?"

"No."

"Is it something I didn't say?"

"No."

"Is it something I did?"

"No."

"Is it something I didn't do?"

"No."

"Is it something I said in casual reference to something I did, when the thing I did shouldn't have been done, or at least done differently with more concern for your feelings?"

"Maybe."

"I knew it."

We may take deep breaths at other times. We can use exercises or techniques so that we breathe better. A doctor may tell us to breathe in or hold our breath. A beautiful scene may take our breath away. Adverts encourage us to use a certain brand of toothpaste to give us fresh breath. A mystic went to the dentist for an extraction and refused an injection because he wanted to transcend dental medication! We would all agree that breathing is vital to life.

Jesus breathed on his disciples and said: "Receive the Holy Spirit." (John 20:22) Scripture connects breath, life and the Holy Spirit. In Genesis 2:7 we read that "the Lord God formed the man from the dust of the ground and breathed into his nostrils the breath of life, and the man became a living being". Psalm 104:30 tells us that "when you [God] send your Spirit, they are created, and you renew the face of the earth".

Job asserts the sovereignty of God in creation: "If it were his intention and he withdrew his spirit and breath, all mankind would perish together and man would return to the dust." (34:14-15) Ezekiel saw a vision of a valley of dry bones (37:1-14). But it was only when the breath of life entered the bones that they stood up and became a vast army (37:10).

God wants to breathe new life, new power, new energy and new strength into us and into his church. His life-giving Spirit restores our souls, renews our strength and refreshes our spirits.

He restores our soul

Perhaps our relationship with God is not as it should be. We may have moved away from God or out of his will. The breath of God – the Spirit of God – wants to blow away the sin and anything that has blocked or obstructed the relationship. He clears out the stuff that has prevented us from breathing properly and living in fellowship with him.

It may be that we are having an argument with God. We may not be talking to him and we are not sure we would like his answer if it came. We do not understand what he is doing or why he has allowed something to happen. Restoring the soul will mean repairing our relationship and resetting our perspective. The breath of God sweeps away the clutter we have accumulated and the wrong thought patterns we have developed and gives us room to breathe so that we can think and see more clearly.

He renews our strength

We may have come to the end of our resources, our strength, our energy or our wisdom. We may even feel we can't do the Christian life any more. We may have got used to shallow breathing by neglecting the reading of God's word and prayer. We are running on empty.

We are told that deep breathing reduces stress, releases chemicals into the system, relieves headaches and stress-related aches and pains, helps to focus the mind and strengthens weak muscles. When we breathe deeply, our lungs expand to absorb the extra oxygen.

Taking in all that God has for us expands our spiritual lungs so that we have more to give to others. Our capacity to worship is enriched, our capacity to love is increased, our capacity to forgive is deepened, and our capacity to serve is enlarged. Why is this? When the power of God is injected into our system, our spiritual muscles are working more efficiently and we draw our strength from his infinite resources. This infusion of strength, this infilling by the Spirit, enables us to live close to God, walk in his ways, know his will and be useful in his service.

The command to "be filled with the Spirit" (Ephesians 5:18) is continuous. It is not a once-and-for-all filling. We leak! We are to go on being filled with the Spirit. We need to breathe in, to take in, the truths of God's word.

Galatians 5:25
Since we live by the Spirit, let us keep in step with the Spirit.

God breathes out his Spirit so that we have everything we need for the Christian life – power to live, love to share, gifts to use and strength to serve.

Fellowship with God means breathing in the pure air of his Spirit, to fill our spiritual lungs and expand our worship, our work and our witness.

He refreshes our spirit

The Holy Spirit brings refreshment and renewal to those parts other things cannot reach. Sometimes we carry burdens of responsibility, care or anxiety. Or it may be a burden of sin and guilt. Perhaps we carry deep burdens or great sadness from the past. Whatever our need, whatever our circumstances, whatever our pain, the Spirit wants to bring healing, wholeness and peace. Perhaps we are weary. There is too much going on and we are unable to cope with the demands upon us.

What did Jesus say? "Come to me, all you who are weary and burdened, and I will give you rest." (Matthew 11:28) This is his invitation to all those who are struggling with the strains and stresses of life and are weighed down by heavy burdens. The Spirit wants to bring refreshment and renewal to our spirits as we come to Jesus and relax in his presence, rest in his love and rely on his strength.

Air quality is monitored because we breathe in what has gone out into the atmosphere. Escaping to the country has a certain appeal to city dwellers, not just for the slower pace of life but for the benefits of getting into the open air. If you like going to the coast, you appreciate the cool air off the sea as you walk along the beach. If you have climbed a mountain, you will have breathed in fresh air. You feel stimulated and reinvigorated and are able to function better because you have taken in good clean air. This is how the Spirit of God works in us as we breathe deeply of the things of God and take in all that God has purposed and planned for us.

The Spirit of God restores our soul, renews our strength and refreshes our spirit. But breathing in is not enough; we need to breathe out what we have received. Living in God's presence and walking in his Spirit should result in us loving liberally, giving generously, forgiving freely and serving sacrificially. By breathing deeply of the Spirit, and running on full rather than empty, we will bring life and hope to those around us who need to know and experience the freshness of God's presence and the pure air of his Spirit.

Chapter Seven

When We Feel We Are Losing The Battle

We all struggle and battle with stuff. However long we have been on the Christian road, we will always face temptation and the fight against sin. It may be a recurring problem (what used to be called a "besetting sin") that we just cannot seem to control. Or perhaps something we once had the mastery of has come back to tell us that the victory we previously enjoyed was not permanent. Or it may be that the pressures and demands on us have made us particularly vulnerable to temptation and through tiredness or weakness we give in and allow ourselves to get caught up in sin that in other circumstances we may have avoided.

But whatever the reason for the failure, defeat or setback, there is a remedy. The writer to the Hebrews gives some helpful and practical advice. The letter was written to Jewish Christians to warn them of the dangers of Judaism, in reverting to their previous way of life with its customs and practices that were inadequate and ineffective. They had come out of legalism into liberty, out of bondage into blessing, into a new covenant and relationship with God secured and sealed by the blood of Jesus. In his death on the cross he made a perfect, complete and final offering for sin that replaced the old system requiring continual and regular sacrifices.

So the challenge to these Christians is to go on with Jesus and not go back to Judaism. The challenge for us is not to get accustomed to defeat but to live in victory with God's help.

Resisting sin

The first verse of Hebrews 12 tells us to "throw off everything that hinders and the sin that so easily entangles".

An illustration of a race is used to describe the Christian life. At the start of a race, athletes do not take with them anything that would slow them down. As part of their preparation and training, they manage their diet, undergo rigorous exercise and develop the right muscles to ensure peak fitness for the event. They do not want to carry excess weight that would interfere with their performance.

Sin "so easily entangles". It affects the way we live and run the race. It affects our mind, our motivation, our strength, our fitness, our development, our relationships – with God and with others. We get caught up in sin when we let down our guard, rely on ourselves and particularly when we fail to wear spiritual armour and use spiritual weapons.

Sin must be resisted. James tells us to "resist the devil, and he will flee from [us]" (4:7b). We must never think we can handle sin or overcome it on our own. We must never say, "That won't happen to me. I won't fall into that sin." Paul reminds us that pride comes before a fall:

> 1 Corinthians 10:12
> *So, if you think you are standing firm, be careful that you don't fall!*

There is no place of permanent victory outside Jesus. He won a decisive and conclusive victory over sin on the cross, but we must appropriate and apply that victory.

Another image used in the New Testament is that of a soldier. We are engaged in spiritual warfare. We have an enemy who will use all possible means to distract us, divert us and defeat us in the Christian life. But we are on the winning side!

> 2 Corinthians 10:4
> *The weapons we fight with are not the weapons of the world. On the contrary, they have divine power to demolish strongholds.*

To share in the victory of Jesus we need to put on, and keep on, our spiritual armour (Ephesians 6:13-18).

The helmet of salvation protects our head and our mind. The breastplate of righteousness covers our heart. The shield of faith enables us to withstand the attacks of the enemy. The sword of the Spirit is the word of God which refutes error through declaring truth. The belt of truth undergirds our lives as people of integrity. The shoes of peace help us to carry the message of the gospel wherever we go. Praying in the Spirit causes us to depend on God's wisdom and strength in overcoming our adversary.

Now back to the race! We must discard those things that hinder us or get in the way. We accumulate so much clutter and baggage in life. The word 'impediment' comes from the Latin word 'impedimenta', the baggage that accompanied Roman soldiers on the march. To make progress in the race, we need to get rid of the stuff that slows us down or holds us back – thought patterns, attitudes, habits, activities or perhaps fear of the unknown.

Running steadfastly

Hebrews 12:1
...let us run with perseverance the race marked out for us.

The Christian life is a marathon, not a sprint. It requires patience and perseverance, motivation and method, energy and enthusiasm. It takes a lifetime to complete. So we should not be discouraged when we fall or stop running. God will pick us up and put us back on track. We need to deal with sin by confessing it and receiving God's forgiveness. Then we should move on.

We are not in competition with other Christians! We must not compare ourselves or compare our gifts with others. We might get elated or disappointed. We start and finish at different times, we run at different speeds and we grow at different rates. What is important is how we run and how we finish. Prizes are given by God to those who run and finish well, for faithful and fruitful service. Our highest motivation is not to work for reward but a desire to please God and for our worship and service to be an expression of our gratitude for his amazing grace.

This is a unique race. We can help others when they fall, slow down or stop running. We can tend their wounds when injured and encourage them to get back into the race. We can lift up our "shield of faith" and pray for them and support them in their own battles and struggles.

The race is "marked out for us". We do not run haphazardly, without direction or guidance. We have the word of God to feed us and the power of the Spirit to fill us as we continue the race.

Raising our sights

Hebrews 12:2
Let us fix our eyes on Jesus, the author and perfecter of our faith...

Jesus has gone before us. He knows the way. We follow him. Our focus and faith must be fixed on Jesus alone. We need to look to him and not to ourselves. There may be things that are painful in our past. We must let go the hurts that we carry and the burden of sad memories. As we give them to God, and release the people who hurt us, we find release ourselves. We saw in chapter 2, when considering the life of Joseph, how the practice of forgiveness brings freedom as we allow God to do his work of grace in us, changing our attitudes and shaping our character.

We all have a history. We thank God for the experiences he has brought us through and for the lessons of faith we have learned. We recognise that every bit of progress and growth is due to his grace. We need to move on and enter into everything that God has purposed and planned for us.

Paul wrote:

> **Philippians 3:13-14**
> *But one thing I do: Forgetting what is behind and straining towards what is ahead, I press on towards the goal to win the prize for which God has called me heavenwards in Christ Jesus.*

When we feel we are losing the battle, we are exhorted to resist sin by wearing our spiritual armour and trusting in the victory that Jesus secured for us on the cross. Running steadfastly requires preparation and perseverance as we run the race and draw our nourishment from God's word and our energy from his

Spirit. And in raising our sights we let go of the past and focus on Jesus who has marked out the way and is with us in every step of our journey of faith.

CHAPTER EIGHT

When There Are No Easy Answers

The question of personal suffering will confront us at some point in life, whether it happens to us or to someone we love. The book of Job does not provide a simple explanation of the mystery of suffering or give a set of easy answers. You will not be able to formulate a nice and neat packaged theology of the problem of pain. But you will discover how God met Job in his suffering and how he took him to a higher level of confidence and faith and a deeper experience of reality and truth.

What happened to Job – how he lost his children, his health and his wealth – is a familiar story. His friends tried to console him; but in linking his suffering to sin they were wide of the mark. He called them "miserable comforters" who made "long-winded speeches" (16:2-3). Much of the book is taken up with a dialogue with his three friends. Then in chapters 38-41 God speaks to him. At the start of the final chapter, we see Job reflecting on what God has shown him and said to him.

Job's short perspective

> Job 42:3b
> *Surely I spoke of things I did not understand,*
> *things too wonderful for me to know.*

Job's perspective was short, his view was limited, his knowledge was incomplete, and his understanding was partial.

Our perspective is set by our position and angle of vision. If you have climbed a hill or mountain, you may have thought you were making progress when you reached the top. But when you get there, you find it is only a ridge and you have more climbing to do! Or your view may be restricted by clouds or mist so that you are unable to see a beautiful scene over a valley.

The famous Charge of the Light Brigade shows the limitations of a short perspective. When Lord Lucan received instructions to advance rapidly, follow the enemy and prevent them from carrying off the guns, it was not just the order that was unclear, but his view was also unclear. He had a short perspective. He was in the valley. The order was issued by Lord Raglan, the army commander, who was six hundred feet above in The Heights.

Lord Raglan had a good view over the plain and a wider perspective on the action. He knew the location and movements of the enemy and that the guns on the redoubts had been captured. But because the order was ambiguous and Lord Lucan's view was limited, the Light Brigade advanced towards the guns at the end of the valley and was caught in crossfire from the hills on one side and the heights on the other side.

> *"Into the valley of death rode the six hundred."*
> *- Tennyson*

We do not see the whole picture or understand the full story of what God is doing with us. Our position determines our perspective and our understanding of reality. We live in time and space. We do not have the capacity to fully grasp the ways and works of God.

Paul sums it up well:

> **Romans 11:33**
> *Oh, the depth of the riches of the wisdom and knowledge of God! How unsearchable his judgments, and his paths beyond tracing out!*

God's sovereign power

We sometimes think of the patience of Job. But God has been patient too, listening to Job as he poured out his soul in the anguish of his suffering.

> **Job 38:1**
> *Then the Lord answered Job out of the storm...*

God does not silence Job, interrupt him, accuse him of unbelief or charge him with sin. He gently and lovingly challenges him about his short perspective and limited understanding. Can Job really expect to know as much as God? Is Job as powerful, as just and as wise as God? He says to him in effect, "Come for a walk." He takes Job on a conducted tour of the universe (38-41) and says to him:

- "Where were you when I laid the earth's foundation?" (38:4a)
- "Have you ever given orders to the morning?" (38:12)
- "Do you know the laws of the heavens?" (38:33a)
- "Do you send the lightning bolts on their way? Do they report to you, Here we are?" (38:35)
- "Do you have an arm like God's, and can your voice thunder like his?" (40:9)

God takes Job on this journey not to make him feel insignificant or inferior but to open his eyes to the wonder of his creation and to see signs of his majesty and might in the structured and orderly world that he designed.

When we do not understand what is going on, when we cannot make sense of what is happening, it is good to remind ourselves of God's faithfulness. God also invites us to explore and enjoy his world with him – the songs of birds, the sounds of the sea, the grandeur of a mountain range, the power of a storm, the colours of a rainbow, the formation of clouds, the design of flowers – and so much more. The writer of Psalm 19 expresses this truth:

> **Psalm 19:1**
> *The heavens declare the glory of God; the skies proclaim the work of his hands.*

All around us we see evidence of his grace and love in the wonder, vastness, beauty, variety, harmony and complexity in nature. God has made himself known in so many ways and supremely in Jesus, who died on the cross to bring us forgiveness from sin and to assure us of eternal life if we trust in him.

We need to let God be God. We cannot contain him, confine him or control him.

When we see God at work and recognise that he is the almighty sovereign Lord of the universe, Lord of creation, Lord of the church and Lord of our lives, we can only come before him in worship.

God's significant purpose

Job said, "My ears had heard of you but now my eyes have seen you." (42:5) Job had let God be God. He had proved he would serve him for nothing, when his prosperity and security had been removed. He emerged from this experience with a deeper faith in God and a humble dependence on him. At the end he was not told the whole story, he did not have perfect understanding, a full explanation or a complete set of answers. He was able to live with the mystery of suffering because he had seen God and that was enough. He was content. He was satisfied.

Job could join with Isaiah and say at the end, "[He gives me] a crown of beauty instead of ashes, the oil of gladness instead of mourning, and a garment of praise instead of a spirit of despair." (Isaiah 61:3)

God had revealed himself to him, spoken to him, reminded him of his power and sovereignty, and reassured him that he was in control. God had met with him and healed his hurts. So God is able to take the broken pieces of our lives and make them into something beautiful for him. He can redeem and use the most adverse, negative and painful circumstances to build confidence, strengthen faith, and draw us closer to him.

> *"For Job, the battleground of faith involved lost possessions, lost family, lost health. We may face a different struggle ... at such times the outer circumstances ... will seem the real struggle ... But the more important struggle takes place inside us. Will we trust God? Job teaches that at the moment when faith is hardest and least likely, then faith is most needed."* [4]
> *- Philip Yancey*

God may not deal with us in the same way as Job. But in times of suffering and in times of doubt and

---

[4] Taken from *Disappointment with God* by Philip Yancey. Copyright © 1988 by Philip Yancey. Used by permission of Zondervan. www.zondervan.com

uncertainty, it is helpful to remember that we have a short perspective. We do not see the whole picture or know the full story, but we can be sure that God is working for our good (Romans 8:28). We need to be reminded of God's sovereign power, that he is in control of the universe and that our lives are in his hands. God has a significant purpose for us to fulfil, that we would know him personally in a relationship and have a closer walk with him. When there are no easy answers to why suffering is allowed, we can say with Job, "My ears had heard of you but now my eyes have seen you." (42:5)

Chapter Nine

When We Are Uncertain About The Way To Go

A student at Bible college decided to miss an afternoon lecture and went shopping in the local town. When he returned, the lecturer asked him why he had missed the class. The student's answer was that the Holy Spirit had told him to go into town to get a book. The lecturer replied, "And did the Holy Spirit also tell you that it is early closing on Wednesday afternoon?"

Guidance is something we all struggle with at some point or at different times in our lives. Can I be sure that God has spoken? Can I be certain that this is the right decision or the right way to go? How can I know God's leading? How do I recognize his guidance?

God has a plan for our lives, and he reveals it to us as we seek his direction and will. This is his promise:

Psalm 32:8
*I will instruct you and teach you in the way you
should go; I will counsel you and watch over you.*

The search for guidance

People today are looking in different places for
guidance. They want to make sense of life. Some read
horoscopes and base their decisions on what they find.
Although there are activities and places that are
forbidden by God's word because of the dangers of the
occult, some will try to find answers by engaging in
these harmful practices.

Some will experiment and explore other religions to
try to find meaning and guidance. Others will try a
'pick and mix' approach in an attempt to discover why
we are here. The view is often taken that all religions
are equally valid as they all contain some truth, and it is
claimed there are different ways of knowing God. 'New
age' philosophy appeals to some people because it
involves looking within ourselves to find harmony and
peace, to be at one with the universe. But none of these
routes will bring clear and reliable guidance that can be
safely trusted as we navigate our way through life.

The source of guidance

Truth and reality are found in God alone. The
Christian faith is unique. It is distinct from other
religions because it is grounded in revelation and grace.
God takes the initiative in revealing himself to us. It is

71

about his search for us rather than our search for him. Jesus said he "came to seek and to save what was lost" (Luke 19:10). It is all about grace – of God giving himself to us in Jesus, a gift we receive by faith.

God primarily guides us through his word. Where there is a clear command to follow, we do not need additional guidance. Where there is no definite instruction or warning, there are principles to guide us as we consider the options open to us. Is this decision honouring to God? Is it something I have pushed for or am I prepared to align my will with God's will? What about my motivation for this thing? Have I set my heart on it or am I prepared to let it go if God says no? What effect will it have on my faith? Will it give me new opportunities to serve and witness?

The Holy Spirit will never tell us to do something that is contrary to Scripture.

The scope of guidance

In addition to his word, the primary source of guidance, God may guide us in a number of ways.

First, we may discern guidance in circumstances. God may open and close doors. This may require a step of faith as we move in a particular direction, when God will confirm the decision, take us in a different direction or close the door. We may sense that God is leading us but need faith to continue the journey, especially when the outcome is unknown. When Abraham was called by God to "go to a place he would later receive as his inheritance, [he] obeyed and went, even though he did not know where he was going" (Hebrews 11:8).

On a journey through Phrygia and Galatia, Paul and his companions were "kept by the Holy Spirit from preaching the word in the province of Asia. When they came to the border of Mysia, they tried to enter Bithynia, but the Spirit of Jesus would not allow them to." (Acts 16:6-7)

Circumstances may work out in such a way that we sense that God is at work. But we need to be careful. Just because something appears to be right does not mean that God arranged it. As we saw in chapter 5, when Jonah decided to run from God because he did not want to preach to the people of Nineveh, he went to Joppa and found a ship going to Tarshish where he was heading (Jonah 1:3). This seemed very convenient!

What about putting out a fleece? When God told Gideon that he would deliver Israel from the Midianites, he asked for two signs – that a wool fleece placed on the ground would be wet and the ground dry, and then that the fleece would be dry and the ground covered with dew (Judges 6:36-40). But God had already told Gideon that he would be with him and that he would strike down the Midianites (Judges 6:16). Gideon acknowledged this:

Judges 6:36
Gideon said to God, "If you will save Israel by my hand as you have promised..."

He did not need extra confirmation, although God graciously accommodated his request. The problem with signs like this is that we want to be in control. We set the conditions for guidance. But we find no other place in Scripture where we are encouraged to put out a fleece. We have the whole revelation of Scripture and the promise of the Holy Spirit to guide us (John 16:13).

What about testing and proving God? In the context of tithing, God said, "Test me in this … and see if I will not throw open the floodgates of heaven and pour out so much blessing that you will not have room enough for it." (Malachi 3:10) This is testing in the sense of proving; putting God to the test is forbidden by Scripture. Jesus was tempted to do this in the desert and each time answered the challenge from Scripture (Matthew 4:1-11):

- "It is written: Man does not live on bread alone, but on every word that comes from the mouth of God." (v.4)
- "It is also written: Do not put the Lord your God to the test." (v.7)
- "For it is written: Worship the Lord your God, and serve him only." (v.10)

Testing God is to deny his word, but proving God is taking him at his word. It is acting in accordance with his word. It is being obedient to his call, moving in faith as God reveals each step or stage of the journey, and trusting him for the outcome.

God expects us to use reasoning and to think through the cost and consequences of decisions and to ask for wisdom when it is needed (James 1:5). With many decisions, we can work out what to do without the need for specific and direct guidance (e.g. what to wear in the morning!) There is such a thing as sanctified common sense.

God may guide us through other Christians. The wise counsel of mature Christians is often helpful. This does not relieve us of our responsibility to make a decision before God but may be useful in clarifying the issues and focusing on what is important.

Prayer is vital as we seek to know and understand the guidance of God. Through prayer we discover and discern God's will. As we listen to him, we discover what is on his heart and we discern where he is leading us, which is usually a gradual process in a series of steps of faith.

God may guide us through our conscience, if this is sensitive to the promptings of the Holy Spirit. We can invite the Spirit to search us and challenge us about anything contrary to his will, so that we remove the barriers and blocks that prevent us from hearing God's voice (Psalm 139:23-24).

In church life, particularly when facing major decisions, it is important to seek consensus and confirmation within the body. Is there agreement about this course of action? God blesses unity within the fellowship (Psalm 133). This will be explored in the next chapter.

The security of guidance

We can safely trust the guidance of God. He will never lead us where his grace cannot keep us. It is possible to be sure, to be clear, to be confident, about his guidance. He has promised to guide those who seek him sincerely.

> **Jeremiah 29:11**
> *"For I know the plans I have for you," declares the Lord, "plans to prosper you and not to harm you, plans to give you hope and a future."*

God may give us a word from Scripture or reveal his will as we pray. We need to ensure our relationship is right and that we are tuned in to listening to his will. He may guide us through circumstances. It may be helpful to discuss a possible decision or check a proposed course of action with other Christians. We can experience a growing sense of conviction about the rightness of a decision. The inner witness of the Holy Spirit confirms what we need to do. We can experience his peace ruling in our hearts (Philippians 4:7), assuring us that we have heard from God and understood what we should do.

God has a plan for our lives, and the more we know him, as our relationship with him deepens and grows, so will we recognize his voice, discern his will and come to the right decision. We will hear his voice saying, "This is the way; walk in it." (Isaiah 30:21)

CHAPTER TEN

When Activity Overtakes Prayer

A man arrived at a vicarage and was met by the teenage son.

"I'm sorry, my father's busy at the moment – he's just had a phone call offering him an industrial chaplaincy."

"But he's only been here two years."

"I know. But he'd get a new car, a big house and a huge salary."

"What's he going to do?"

"Don't know. He's in the study praying for guidance."

"And your mother?"

"Oh, she's upstairs packing."[5]

---

[5] From *Bats in the Belfry* by Murray Watts. Copyright © Murray Watts 1989. Minstrel Monarch Publications. Used by permission.

Finding a balance between prayer and action is not easy. For many of us, activity appeals to us because we feel we are making an effort and doing something useful whereas prayer requires us to slow down in an attitude of stillness and quiet so that we hear from God. It is actually more useful to discover God's plans and timing before making important decisions or moving in a particular direction. This does not remove or reduce the need for faith as the details or outcome may be unknown and guidance may be revealed in stages. But it is vital to know that our decisions and plans carry God's endorsement and blessing.

The example of Nehemiah is instructive and shows how prayer and action combine when priorities are set and the will of God is sought at the beginning. The people of Israel had been taken into captivity to Babylon, as prophesied in Scripture. But God also declared they would return (Isaiah 45). Cyrus, the Persian king, overthrew the Babylonian empire and allowed the Israelites to go home.

Nehemiah is in the king's service in Persia. He receives news of the condition of the people in Jerusalem and the state of the city walls.

Nehemiah 1:3
...Those who survived the exile and are back in the province are in great trouble and disgrace. The wall of Jerusalem is broken down, and its gates have been burned with fire.

What is his reaction?

Nehemiah 1:4
When I heard these things, I sat down and wept.
For some days I mourned and fasted and prayed
before the God of heaven.

Prayer precedes action

We see the relationship of prayer to action. Prayer comes first. Nehemiah could have formulated a plan, suggested a course of action to others or appealed to the king at this point. But instead he sought God in prayer.

This took four months! God is never in a hurry. His timing and purposes are perfect. We may need to wait for God's answer because we are not ready or others in the plan of God are not ready or in place. God brings all the pieces together and all the parties into position at the right time, the time that suits his purpose. So seeking him in prayer to discover and discern his will is vital before moving ahead.

Prayer prepares for action

While we are waiting for God to speak or guide us, several things may happen:

* We invite God to examine us, to deal with sin or anything that would prevent us from knowing or doing his will.

Psalm 139:23-24
Search me, O God, and know my heart; test me
and know my anxious thoughts. See if there is

any offensive way in me, and lead me in the way everlasting.

- There may be a need to confess sin, to get right with God. Nehemiah identified himself with the people's sin and rebellion.

Nehemiah: 1:6b-7
I confess the sins we Israelites, including myself and my father's house, have committed against you. We have acted very wickedly towards you. We have not obeyed the commands, decrees and laws you gave your servant Moses.

- We submit our ideas and thinking to God, not presenting him with a preconceived plan to bless or a predetermined programme to endorse. (We saw in chapter 4 that David had a good idea, to build a temple for God, contrary to God's plan. But with Nehemiah, God put the idea of the building project in his heart.)

Nehemiah 2:12
...I had not told anyone what my God had put in my heart to do for Jerusalem.

How do we know if God has put something into our heart, that an idea is not just a product of our thinking or a projection of our imagination?

- We should check our motives. Will this thing honour and glorify God? Do I really desire this for the growth and advancement of his kingdom?

- Do I sense in my spirit this is from God? Do I have a witness of the Spirit? He is the Spirit of truth who will not contradict God's revealed word in Scripture.
- Do I have increasing assurance this is from God, a growing conviction that he has placed this desire in my heart?
- Has God prepared and equipped me for a particular task? Do I sense he is leading in a particular direction?
- Is there confirmation from other Christians or from my church family? Is there agreement about a course of action?
- Does God's peace rule in my heart, settling the issue beyond doubt?

Prayer prompts action

Nehemiah was the king's cupbearer. It was his job to taste the wine. This was a trusted position. He comes before the king who asks him, "Why the long face?" (Nehemiah 2:2, The Message). It was not a good thing to be sad in the king's presence!

"With a quick prayer to the God of heaven" (Nehemiah 2:4, TLB), Nehemiah explains his concerns to the king. He is allowed to go to Jerusalem with the king's authority, under the king's protection and with the provision of building materials.

An 'arrow prayer', as used by Nehemiah, is short and spontaneous, expressing an immediate or urgent need. This may be for something practical, for guidance or direction about what to do, or how to react to a person or situation. It may be a prayer for protection or provision. Or God may bring the name of someone to us at a particular moment for us to pray. We may not know the details but we lift them to God in prayer, asking him to meet their need and bless them. Or we may have just received news that prompts us to pray for God to bring healing and peace for someone who is suffering.

Because God had put the desire to build into Nehemiah's heart, the plans began to take shape in his mind. There were three parts to this process:

ASSESSMENT

Nehemiah surveyed the city walls. He wanted accurate information about their condition, where they would need strengthening and where there were vulnerable parts where attack would be likely.

> Nehemiah 4:9
> *But we prayed to our God and posted a guard day and night to meet this threat.*

Prayer and posting went together. The building project was birthed and bathed in prayer, but then there was a need for action.

When God puts a desire in our hearts, it calls for action, a response or a decision. What is God calling me to do? What has he prepared and equipped me to do? Where is he leading me? What is he showing me?

Seeking God for guidance and direction does not remove our responsibility to think about the options available and the implications and consequences of decisions. Like Nehemiah, it may be necessary to gather information so that a decision is based on relevant facts.

For example, if we are preparing for a job interview it would be prudent to do some research about the company or organisation that we would like to join! Moving house will require investigation about an area to which we feel called to move, and we will need to know about transport links to a workplace, schools for children, proximity to shops and of course the churches in the locality. And in looking for a new church, God expects us to apply our minds as we consider different styles of worship, the nature of the teaching and preaching programme, the extent of their witness and engagement with their community. In looking at the size and mix of a congregation, it would be helpful to know the scope for using our gifts and the opportunities for service. As we pray and think through what God has placed on our heart, he will make clear the right course of action to follow.

ASSISTANCE

Nehemiah included and involved everyone in the building programme. Shallum repaired a section of the wall with the help of his daughters (Nehemiah 3:12). The vision given by God to Nehemiah had to be shared and embraced by the people so that there were sufficient people available with their different gifts and resources to contribute to the task.

> **Nehemiah 2:18**
> *I also told them about the gracious hand of my God upon me and what the king had said to me. They replied, "Let us start rebuilding." So they began this good work.*

Before making a major decision, or engaging in a new form of service, we may seek the counsel of others to check that we are hearing from God correctly. In the context of church life, it is possible to be caught up with activity and not take time out to seek God about the effectiveness and continuation of a programme or whether a fresh approach is required. God may call us to start or assist with a new ministry to engage with the community or meet a particular need. What is important here is consensus and confirmation to ensure that the vision is received and agreed by the fellowship. This provides encouragement and support when obstacles arise and the going is tough. It also ensures the contribution of different gifts, the sharing of responsibility and accountability within the group that has been called by God and the church to implement and oversee the programme.

ASSURANCE

Nehemiah's confidence was in God. The people had to do the work, but God's hand was on the project to guarantee its completion. The opposition would be overcome as the people worked and trusted in God. The project is described as a "good work", and the hand of God is not only on our work but also on us (Nehemiah 2:18).

- Prayer precedes action – prayer should come first before we move ahead and make decisions.
- Prayer prepares for action – as we open ourselves to God and submit to his will.
- Prayer prompts action – as we discern and discover God's will and our part in his plan, so we move forward confident in his power to guide and lead us.

  "As you wait upon the Lord, you learn to see things from His perspective, move at His pace, and function under His directives.

  Waiting times are growing times and learning times,

  As you quiet your heart you enter His peace

  As you sense your weakness you receive His strength

  As you lay down your will, you hear His calling

  When you mount up, you are being lifted by the wind of His Spirit

  When you move ahead, you are sensitive to His timing

When you act, you give yourself only to the things He has asked you to do. [6]

- *Roy Lessin*

CHAPTER ELEVEN

When We Are Not Sure If We Will Make It

It is possible to try to derive our assurance about our standing with God from our own efforts and perseverance. But what happens if we stop running and drop out of the race? What is the result if we think we have blown it and can never be forgiven and restored? What if we think we have committed the "unpardonable sin"? Is there no way back to God? Is there no hope for us? Have we reached the point of no return?

Paul has some encouraging words for us in chapter 8 of his letter to the Christians in Rome. He sets out the truth that it is our position in Christ that determines our security on which our confidence and assurance should be based.

The conviction expressed

Romans 8:28

And we know that in all things God works for the good of those who love him, who have been called according to his purpose.

The emphasis is on God working "in all things" rather than the things working themselves out. The fact that God allows something to happen does not mean that he caused it to happen, but he is able to use it for his purpose.

God is working for our good, our spiritual benefit and advantage. It does not mean we sit back and do nothing. Paul encourages us to work out our salvation "for it is God who works in you to will and to act according to his good purpose" (Philippians 2:12-13). This has nothing to do with working *for* salvation, of seeking to find or receive salvation through good works, effort or merit. Salvation is the gift of God. It is a gift of grace, received by faith (see Ephesians 2:8). But when salvation has been received, the works should follow (Ephesians 2:10). So we should work *out* what God has first worked *in* to our lives. It is often said that if we supply the willingness, God supplies the power.

Jeremiah writes of a visit to the potter's house, where he sees the potter at work on his wheel:

Jeremiah 18:4

But the pot he was shaping from the clay was marred in his hands; so the potter formed it into another pot, shaping it as seemed best to him.

There was some defect or flaw in the pot. But the potter did not discard or destroy it – the pot was going to be something better. He reworked and reshaped it, making it into something useful and useable. God does this with us. He is at work in our failures and mistakes, weaving them into his purposes and plans.

In Romans 8 we find the word "predestined":

Romans 8:29
For those God foreknew he also predestined to be conformed to the likeness of his Son, that he might be the firstborn among many brothers.

The doctrine of predestination has generated much controversy and sometimes more heat than light! It is concerned with what God has purposed and planned for us and our direction and destiny as Christians. God had his hand upon us before we were born.

Psalm 139:13-16a
For you created my inmost being; you knit me together in my mother's womb. I praise you because I am fearfully and wonderfully made; your works are wonderful, I know that full well. My frame was not hidden from you when I was made in the secret place. When I was woven together in the depths of the earth, your eyes saw my unformed body.

If ever you feel unloved, inadequate or insignificant, read Psalm 139 which will reassure you of God's interest and care for you!

God takes all the circumstances and experiences of life and uses them to conform us to the likeness of Jesus (see Romans 8:29). As we have previously considered, we are work in progress and can be sure that God will complete the good work begun in us (Philippians 1:6).

The confidence to be enjoyed

The confidence comes from knowing that God is on our side. He is "for us" (Romans 8:31). God is with us, in us and for us! Selwyn Hughes puts it like this:

> *"God is for us against our sin, not against us for our sin."*[7]

We are justified, made right with God, through the redeeming and atoning sacrifice of Jesus on the cross.

Romans 8:33
Who will bring any charge against those whom God has chosen? It is God who justifies.

It used to be the case in England and Wales that under the 'double jeopardy' rule, someone acquitted of a crime could not be tried again for the same offence. That rule has been repealed and it is possible for someone to be prosecuted again if there is fresh and compelling evidence likely to lead to a conviction.

We have been acquitted of our sin, and when it is forgiven it will never again be raised by God for he remembers it no more (Isaiah 43:25). He does not

---

[7] From *Every Day with Jesus* by Selwyn Hughes, published by CWR. Copyright © CWR. Used by permission.

forget our sin but chooses to erase it from his memory. Paul has already stated that there is no condemnation for those who are in Christ Jesus, for they have been released by the law of the Spirit of life from the law of sin and death (Romans 8:1-2).

Paul is not saying that we can continue sinning or that sin does not matter. He disposed of that argument in an earlier chapter of his letter:

Romans 6:1-2
What shall we say, then? Shall we go on sinning, so that grace may increase? By no means! We died to sin; how can we live in it any longer?

In chapter 8, Paul is thinking of our legal status before God. He is saying we are no longer condemned for our sin because of what Jesus accomplished on the cross and his resurrection which validated his sacrifice to God. He paid the price and bore the penalty for our sin so that we will not be charged and condemned. We have been made right with God – justification; now we need to keep right with God – sanctification. Justification refers to our standing and position in Christ and sanctification refers to our relationship and walk with him, the process of being conformed to his likeness (Romans 8:29).

But there is more! We have an advocate who represents us and pleads on our behalf in heaven. The prayers of Jesus are always answered because they are backed by his perfect faith and obedience.

Romans 8:34
*Who is he that condemns? Christ Jesus, who died
– more than that, who was raised to life – is at
the right hand of God and is also interceding for
us.*

This truth is illustrated in the letter to the Hebrews
as the writer focuses on the continuing and effective
ministry of Jesus in heaven:

Hebrews 7:24b-25
*...because Jesus lives for ever, he has a permanent
priesthood. Therefore he is able to save
completely those who come to God through him,
because he always lives to intercede for them.*

Remember what Jesus said to Peter? "But I have
prayed for you, Simon, that your faith may not fail"
(Luke 22:32a). Peter denied and betrayed his Lord but
was forgiven and restored and used to help build the
church after he was empowered by the Holy Spirit. His
faith did not ultimately fail, because of the promise and
prayer of Jesus. We can be confident our sins are
forgiven and we are no longer under condemnation for
the things we have done or the way we have lived.

The conquest to be experienced

Nothing can sever us from the love of God secured
to us in Christ (Romans 8:35,38-39). We can experience victory in all our circumstances for "we are
more than conquerors through him who loved us"
(Romans 8:37).

This is not about denial of reality or escapism. It is not about pretending everything is fine when our hearts are breaking, when we are in pain or when we are grieving over the loss of a loved one or the loss of something precious to us. It is saying that we will not be defined by our circumstances, our condition, our health, our feelings or whatever else seeks to control or bind us. We are not exempt or immune from suffering or hardship. The tests and the trials will come. We will know failure and disappointment. But we need not be overcome or overwhelmed by them for we have the life and power of God within us by his Spirit. He is working for our good "in all things" (Romans 8:28).

We can be victors and not victims. A victim is unable to control what happens to them. But God says to us that we need not be defined by what happens, we need not be defeated by what happens or diminished by what happens. The victory is in the circumstances, in the "all things" that are part of life and included in the journey of faith. There is victory over sin, guilt, temptation, fear, anxiety and whatever comes that would rob us of our peace.

The conviction expressed is that we can be sure that God is working in all our circumstances and experiences for our good and to fulfil his purpose in building his kingdom.

The confidence to be enjoyed is that we can know the assurance of sins forgiven through the complete work of Jesus on the cross and his continuing ministry in heaven.

The conquest to be experienced is that we can be certain of the victory in whatever we face, for Jesus has defeated every power that seeks to overcome us and nothing can separate us from his love.

CHAPTER TWELVE

When We Need To
Rediscover Our Hope

The personal and visible return of Jesus Christ is clearly taught in the Bible. When Paul wrote his letters to the Christians in Thessalonica, he thanked God for their productive faith, their powerful witness and their patient endurance in the face of suffering. This was evidence of authentic Christian living and proof that God was at work among them.

Some of these believers thought that Jesus would return soon and had given up work to wait for him. There was a concern too about Christians who had died and what had happened to them. So Paul explains the hope that every believer in Christ enjoys, and for us who are alive this is not an invitation to sit back and take life easy but an incentive to work hard and please him through faithful and fruitful service.

The hope of the Christian is not a vague and unreliable belief about our eternal destiny.

It is a sure hope – providing security

Imagine you are taking part in the television programme 'Who wants to be a millionaire?' You are on the final question. You stand to win one million pounds. You are stuck on this question. It could be on any subject – religion, history, geography, literature, food, films or sport. But you have a friend who is very knowledgeable, and you are very confident he will know the answer. So you call him and take the answer he gives you – which is right!

You do this because:

- You have known him for a long time and he has been a good friend.
- You trust his wisdom and knowledge.
- His advice in the past has always been reliable.
- He is a person of integrity and would not mislead you by giving a wrong answer.

When God tells us that we have a secure hope and that Jesus will return for his people and with his people, and that all those who belong to him will be with him for eternity, we know this is true and reliable. What is the basis for this hope?

- We have experienced God in relationship, perhaps for many years.
- We trust his supreme wisdom and knowledge.

- He has been faithful in the past and we have proved his power in a range of circumstances.
- We have found his nature and character to be loving and good, and we can depend on the integrity of his word and promises.

If Paul had been asked about his hope in Jesus, about whether he was sure he was a Christian, or whether he would get to heaven, what would he have said? "I assume so"? Or "I think so"? Or "I believe so"? Or "I hope so"? This is what he wrote to Timothy:

2 Timothy 1:12
...I know whom I have believed, and am convinced that he is able to guard what I have entrusted to him for that day.

The conviction, confidence and commitment which underpin this statement of faith may be experienced by all those who belong to Jesus. On the authority of God's word, we may know with certainty that if we trust in the finished work of Jesus on the cross, when he died to rescue and redeem us from sin, and we commit our lives to him, we will be with him when he returns for his people.

It is a satisfying hope – creating comfort

Grief is natural and right when we lose someone we love. We would be less than human if we did not grieve over the loss of a loved one. Jesus was deeply moved with compassion and wept at the tomb of his friend Lazarus (John 11:35).

Must we "walk in black and go sadly, with longdrawn faces"[8]? We do not "grieve like the rest of men, who have no hope" (1 Thessalonians 4:13). In the midst of our sadness and pain, we are reassured by the knowledge that those who have died knowing Jesus as their Saviour and Lord will be with us in eternity. We will see them again. They enjoy the security of the same hope that we have, and this is the privilege of everyone who belongs to Jesus. We have a living hope, guaranteed by the resurrection of Jesus who is alive today and is seated at the right hand of God where he intercedes for us.

1 Thessalonians 4:14
We believe that Jesus died and rose again and so we believe that God will bring with Jesus those who have fallen asleep in him.

So while we miss those we love, and rightly mourn for them, we may be comforted by these truths and need not be overwhelmed by sadness or overcome by grief.

---

[8] From *Selected Poems* by T. S. Eliot. Copyright © T. S. Eliot 1954. Faber and Faber. Used by permission.

It is a sanctifying hope – encouraging holiness

We want to be ready and prepared for the return of Jesus, not just because we want to receive his commendation for faithful and fruitful service but because we want to please him who gave everything for us.

> 1 John 3:2.3
> *...But we know that when he appears, we shall be like him, for we shall see him as he is. Everyone who has this hope in him purifies himself, just as he is pure.*

Justification ("just as if I'd never sinned") concerns our legal, external position with God. He makes us righteous, *declares* us righteous, on the basis of the atoning and redeeming work of Jesus on the cross. The righteousness of Jesus is credited to our account (Romans 4:5).

Abraham Lincoln was asked about how he would treat the rebellious southerners after the American Civil War had ended. He replied, "I am going to treat them as if they had never been away." This is how God treats us when he justifies us and makes things right between us.

Sanctification concerns our relationship with God. It is a love relationship, not a legal one. It is family, not forensic. It is internal, not external. Sanctification is the process of becoming like Jesus, in our thinking, our attitudes, our motives, our reactions, our character and our conduct. Holiness is about displaying a distinctive and different lifestyle that honours God, by the power and energy of the Holy Spirit.

Our relationship, our walk with God, needs to be maintained and nurtured. This used to be called "keeping short accounts with God". Repentance is a change of mind, accompanied by a change of heart, expressed in a change of direction. It is saying, "I am wrong." It is agreeing with God.

We fail and fall but there is always a way back to God, and a way forward with God, through confession of sin. The hope that we have of seeing Jesus face to face should keep us close to him now so that we will not be sad because of the way we have lived or be ashamed when he returns in glory.

> **2 Peter 3:11-12**
> *Since everything will be destroyed in this way, what kind of people ought you to be? You ought to live holy and godly lives as you look forward to the day of God and speed its coming...*

It is a stimulating hope – motivating service

We are not called to be "so heavenly minded that we are of no earthly use". We need our feet on the ground and our hearts in heaven.

> **Colossians 3:1**
> *Since, then, you have been raised with Christ, set your hearts on things above, where Christ is seated at the right hand of God.*

But as well as having an eternal perspective, our feet need to be planted firmly on the ground. Did you know that you have beautiful feet? You might say, "You haven't seen my feet"! Paul tells us that those who bring good news have beautiful feet (Romans 10:15). This is because they carry a beautiful message – that God so loved the world that he gave his only Son Jesus to save us from our sin (John 3:16). The hope that we enjoy moves us to pray and work to see the kingdom of God grow and extend on earth. We are grateful for grace received, motivated by mercy given. And so we have good news to bring to our hungry, hurting world – a message of hope. Although our work and service is here on earth, it has eternal significance and results.

In his Introduction, in The Message, to Paul's letters to the Thessalonian Christians, Eugene Peterson writes:

> *"The practical effect of this belief is to charge each moment of the present with hope."*

If you have experienced a flat battery in your car, you will know the benefit of charging! It releases power, life and energy. And so our hope should empower and energise us as we tell of the redeeming and reconciling love of God in Jesus, who will return to this earth to rule and reign in power and glory.

We have a sure hope providing security, backed by the faithfulness of God's nature, the consistency of his character and the integrity of his word. We have a satisfying hope, creating comfort as we trust in the promise of Jesus that death is not the end and we shall be with him for ever. We have a sanctifying hope, encouraging holiness as we seek to live right and please him by our lives. And we have a stimulating hope that motivates us to serve and to see his kingdom grow as we share the good news with those around us.

Conclusion

The theme of this book is that although disappointment, discouragement and defeat may occur, the Christian life is not controlled or defined by external events or internal tensions. Rather, it is a life of faith and trust where our confidence is in God and not in ourselves and where we find forgiveness in his unlimited grace, draw strength from his infinite resources and set our hope on his unchanging purposes.

We have a story to tell of a God who is rich in mercy and who loves us so much that he sent his Son to die on a cross to save us from our sin. The story may be punctuated by failure and setback, but God will complete the work he has begun in our lives. And new chapters are written as other people read our story and come to faith in God through hearing of his love for them and seeing the changes he has brought about in us.

The journey of faith is a real and true story of how we encounter God in all the circumstances and experiences of life. It is about learning the practice of forgiveness and finding release in letting go of our hurts and pain. It is about handling the times when God seems to be remote or silent and resting in his love when our plans collapse or the answers do not come.

In this journey God will renew and refresh us by his Spirit when we are weary or exhausted or think that we cannot do the Christian life any more. If we run from him or feel that the responsibility given is too much for us, God pursues us in love to gently draw us back into his good purpose and will. Although feelings are unreliable, faith is dependable as we hold on to the sure promises of God in his word and trust him to guide us when the way is unclear or the future is uncertain. Faith is about a growing relationship with God, connecting with him in prayer and discerning his will before making major decisions. It is the recognition that failure is not final and we are on the winning side through the victory gained by Jesus on the cross. And finally, it is having a secure hope in God that stimulates and motivates us to serve him well, not to earn his approval but to express our gratitude for his amazing grace.

Suggestions for Further Reading

Bruce, F.F. (1981) *The New Testament Documents: Are They Reliable?*, 6th edition, The Inter-Varsity Fellowship, Leicester

Forster, R. & Marston, P. (1989) *Reason and Faith*, Monarch Publications, Eastbourne

Hybels, B. (1988) *Too Busy Not To Pray*, Inter-Varsity Press, Leicester

Kendall, R.T. (1978) *Jonah*, Hodder & Stoughton, London

Kendall, R.T. (2003) *God Meant it for Good*, Authentic Classics, Milton Keynes

Lewis, C.S. (2012) *Mere Christianity*, C.S. Lewis Signature Classics Edition, HarperCollins Publishers, London

Lloyd, M. (2009) *Café Theology*, Alpha International, London

Lloyd-Jones, D.M. (1965) *Spiritual Depression,* Pickering & Inglis, London

MacDonald, G. (2004) *Rebuilding Your Broken World*, Thomas Nelson, Nashville, USA

Packer, J.I. (1975) *Knowing God*, Hodder & Stoughton, London

Warren, R. (2002) *The Purpose-Driven Life*, Zondervan, Michigan, USA

Yancey, P. (2001) *Soul Survivor*, Hodder & Stoughton, London